MOTHER

"If you were to ask what is most important in a home, I would say memories." Lillian Gish

For _____

From _____

And so it begins...

Your date and place of birth:

_____

_____

Your parents' names, birthdates, and places of birth:

_____

_____

_____

_____

_____

_____

Your brothers and sisters, from oldest to youngest:

_____

_____

_____

_____

_____

_____

_____

How did your parents choose your name?

_____

_____

_____

_____

_____

_____

_____

_____

Childhood...

Which memories from your youngest years stand out?

_____

_____

_____

_____

_____

_____

_____

_____

_____

_____

_____

_____

_____

_____

_____

_____

_____

_____

_____

_____

_____

What kind of child were you?

_____

_____

WHAT ONE LOVES IN CHILDHOOD STAYS IN THE HEART FOREVER.

_____
_____
_____
_____
_____
_____
_____
_____

_____
_____
_____
_____
_____
_____
_____
_____
_____
_____

Me!

What do you remember about your mom and dad?

_____

_____

_____

_____

_____

_____

_____

_____

_____

_____

_____

_____

Mom & dad

What did your mom and dad do for a living?

Where did your family go on VACATION ?

What were your favorite foods?

What was the family car? What do you remember most about it?

_____

_____

_____

_____

_____

Were there any magical places in your childhood home you remember?

_____

_____

_____

_____

_____

_____

_____

_____

_____

_____

_____

What was your room like?

_____

_____

_____

_____

_____

_____

_____

_____

_____

Did you keep your room clean? (Of course you did!)

_____

_____

_____

_____

_____

_____

_____

_____

LIFE IS GOOD

Did you have pets? Tell me about them.

A SOFT FURRY WARM TOASTY
FRIENDLY LITTLE PETTY-PET
OF YOUR OWN IS A MUST ♥.

Your Family Pet

Did you help out around the house? Did you get an allowance?

_____

_____

_____

_____

_____

Did you have other ways of earning money?

_____

_____

_____

_____

_____

_____

_____

_____

_____

_____

_____

_____

_____

_____

What were your favorite pastimes?

What was your favorite childhood book?

_____

_____

_____

_____

_____

_____

_____

_____

_____

What were your favorite TV shows?

_____

_____

_____

_____

_____

_____

_____

_____

_____

_____

_____

_____

Describe your favorite outfit.

_____
_____
_____
_____
_____
_____
_____
_____
_____
_____
_____
_____

What were your favorite accessories?

_____
_____
_____
_____
_____
_____
_____
_____
_____

What were your favorite games?

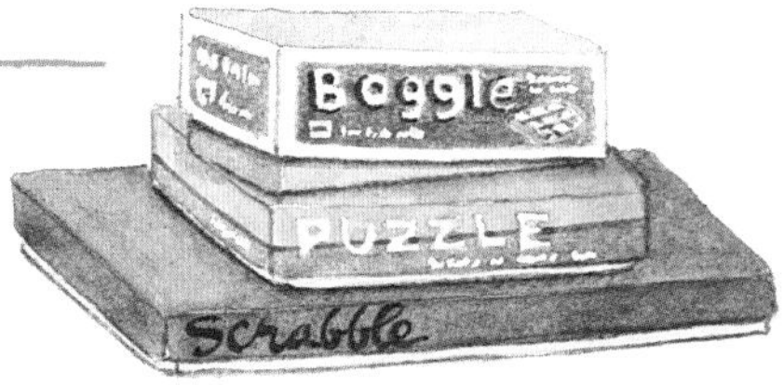

Describe a favorite toy.

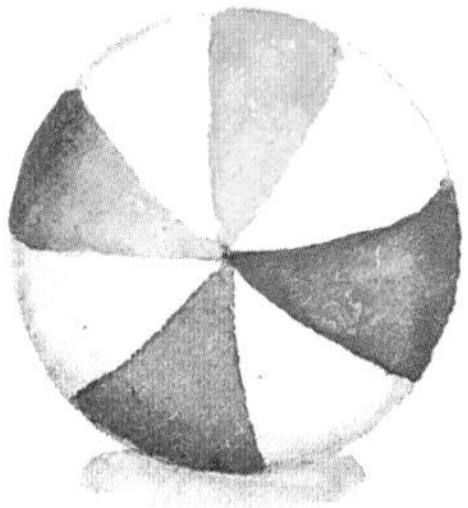

Who were your childhood friends?

_____

_____

_____

_____

_____

_____

_____

_____

_____

_____

_____

_____

Where did they live?

_____

_____

_____

_____

_____

When did you first spend the night at a friend's house? Were you scared?

_____

_____

_____

_____

_____

_____

Tell me a sleepover story from that time.

_____

_____

_____

_____

_____

_____

_____

_____

_____

_____

_____

_____

memories are made of this ♥.

What was your first school?

_____

_____

_____

_____

_____

_____

_____

Who was your favorite elementary school teacher, and why?

_____

_____

_____

_____

_____

_____

_____

_____

_____

Describe a typical school day.

_____

_____

_____

_____

_____

_____

_____

_____

School days

Did you participate in any special school events?

What did you do during the summer?

_____

_____

_____

_____

_____

_____

_____

_____

_____

_____

_____

_____

_____

_____

_____

_____

_____

_____

_____

_____

Did you play make-believe? What did you like to pretend?

Describe a typical Saturday.

Tell me a FAMILY story or two…

Remember...

♥ Special Times ♥

Growing up...

What did you dream about while growing up?

_____
_____
_____
_____
_____
_____
_____
_____
_____
_____
_____
_____
_____
_____
_____
_____
_____
_____
_____
_____
_____

Memories . . . the food of our childhood, food that meant love. ♥

Did you like school?

_____

_____

_____

_____

How did you get to school?

_____

_____

_____

_____

_____

Picture Perfect

How did you get ready for school? What did you wear?

glue photo
here

Did you use makeup? Nail polish?

_____
_____
_____
_____
_____

How did you do your hair?

_____
_____
_____
_____
_____
_____
_____
_____
_____
_____
_____

SMART,
PRETTY
& TALENTED...

What was your favorite subject, and why?

WHAT ONE LOVES IN CHILDHOOD STAYS IN THE HEART FOREVER

Which teacher inspired you the most?

_____

_____

_____

_____

_____

_____

_____

_____

Which teacher do you wish you had stood up to?

_____

_____

_____

_____

_____

_____

_____

_____

_____

_____

_____

Did you belong to any school clubs?

Were you on any sports teams? Tell me about an important game.

TEAM
picture

Did you ever ditch school?

_____

_____

_____

_____

_____

_____

_____

What was the worst thing you got in trouble for in high school?

_____

_____

_____

_____

_____

_____

_____

_____

_____

_____

_____

_____

What was the biggest thing you remember happening in our country when you were in high school?

_____

_____

_____

_____

_____

_____

_____

Did you pay attention to politics or what was going on in the world?

_____

_____

_____

_____

_____

_____

_____

_____

_____

_____

_____

Did you keep a diary or journal then? Do you still have it?

Did you make money in high school? How?

Who taught you how to drive? What was that like?

_____

_____

_____

_____

_____

_____

_____

_____

Tell me about getting your driver's license.

_____

_____

_____

_____

_____

_____

_____

_____

_____

_____

_____

_____

_____

What was your first car?

How much did a gallon of gas cost then? Did you do a lot of driving?

sing IN THE CAR

Did you go to dances and parties? What were they like?

_____

_____

_____

_____

_____

_____

_____

_____

_____

What did everyone wear?

_____

_____

_____

_____

_____

_____

_____

_____

HAPPINESS! HA-CHA-CHA! ♥ Louis Armstrong

How did everyone dance, or did they? What was the music like?

GOOD ♥ FRIENDS

Who was your best friend?

_____

_____

How did you meet?

_____

_____

_____

_____

_____

_____

_____

_____

Tell me about a best friend adventure.

_____

_____

_____

_____

_____

_____

_____

_____

_____

_____

_____

_____

_____

_____

_____

_____

_____

_____

_____

_____

_____

What was your social life like?

_____

_____

_____

_____

_____

_____

_____

_____

Who did you hang out with the most?

_____

_____

_____

_____

_____

_____

_____

_____

_____

_____

_____

_____

Tell me about something that made you laugh until you cried.

_____

_____

_____

_____

_____

_____

_____

_____

_____

_____

_____

_____

_____

_____

_____

_____

_____

_____

FUNNY STUFF

You were sooooo funny!

Tell me about your first date. (Who was your date? Where did you go? How old were you? What did you do? Do you remember what you wore? Details please, Mom.)

Did you like fashion magazines? If not, what did you read for fun?

Who were your favorite movie stars? Movies?

How about music? What did you like? ♪♫ ♪♫ ♪♫ ♪♫

_____

_____

_____

_____

_____

_____

_____

_____

What was your favorite song, and why?

_____

_____

_____

_____

_____

_____

_____

_____

_____

_____

_____

_____

_____

_____

Did you go to concerts? Tell me about your favorite ones.

♫♪♫
OH HAPPY DAY!

What did you have then that we don't use anymore?

What was an exciting invention of the day?

As you matured, what kinds of things inspired you?

Tell me about your high school dreams.

Do you use anything you learned in high school in your grown-up life?

How are you the same now as you were when you were a teenager?

_____

_____

_____

_____

_____

_____

_____

_____

_____

_____

_____

_____

_____

_____

_____

_____

_____

KEEPING A
POSITIVE
ATTITUDE

On your own . . .

Did you ever think about what kind of house you wanted someday?

Or where you might live?

How old were you when you moved out of the house? Where did you go?

What was your place like? Did you live alone?

_____

_____

_____

_____

_____

_____

_____

_____

_____

_____

_____

_____

_____

_____

_____

_____

_____

_____

_____

_____

_____

_____

How did you like being on your own?

_____

_____

_____

_____

_____

_____

_____

_____

What did you miss most from living at home?

_____

_____

_____

_____

_____

_____

_____

_____

_____

_____

When did you first feel like a grown-up?

What was your first job? How much did you make? What did you do?

What was your worst job ever?

Which job did you like best, and why?

_____

_____

_____

_____

_____

_____

_____

_____

_____

_____

_____

_____

_____

_____

_____

_____

_____

_____

_____

_____

What did you do for fun?

_____

_____

_____

_____

_____

_____

_____

_____

_____

_____

_____

_____

_____

_____

_____

_____

_____

FUN is GOOD. ♥ _____

Did you take any big trips?

Share some stories from that time.

Perfect
Day

Write a page or two about the loves in your life. Start at the beginning, please.

You are the sunshine of my life! xx

SWEETHEARTS

(COO)

Did you ever experience love at first sight? Did it work out?

Tell me about the most romantic date you ever went on.

MR. WONDERFUL

Write about the one that got away.

Fragile

WILDFLOWER

I found it on
my walk this
morning — out
in the woods,
all by itself.

The seeds are
slow to spread so
we never pick them —
enjoy them where
they sit.

Lady's Slipper
unpredictable)

means 'Capricious (fickle or
Beauty' in flower language.

LADY'S SLIPPER

SPOTTED IN THE WOODS
June 19TH

Martha's Vineyard

Starting a family...

Write about my dad. Tell me how you met him.

_____

_____

_____

_____

_____

_____

_____

_____

_____

_____

_____

_____

_____

_____

_____

_____

_____

_____

_____

_____

_____

_____

Mom & Dad

Tell me about your first home together.

_____

_____

_____

_____

_____

_____

_____

_____

_____

_____

_____

_____

_____

LIFE IS GOOD

What is your best advice about relationships?

"Love is friendship set to music."
Anonymous ♥

Did you work? How was that part of your life going?

Tell me about finding out you were going to have me.

_____

_____

_____

_____

_____

_____

_____

_____

_____

_____

_____

_____

_____

_____

_____

_____

_____

_____

_____

_____

_____

(I'm pregnant!)

Who did you tell first?

How were those nine months?

A LADY-IN-WAITING

Based on your pregnancy, did you have any ideas about what kind of person I would be?

Did you like to eat anything interesting while you were pregnant?

_____

_____

_____

_____

_____

_____

_____

_____

_____

What was your favorite maternity outfit?

_____

_____

_____

_____

_____

_____

_____

_____

_____

On the day I was born…

How did it feel the first time you held me?

_____

_____

_____

_____

_____

_____

_____

_____

_____

_____

_____

_____

_____

_____

_____

_____

_____

_____

_____

_____

Me! ♥

How was I most challenging as a baby?

What is your favorite story from when I was a baby?

How did your own mom, my grandma, affect your motherhood?

_____

_____

_____

_____

_____

_____

_____

_____

_____

_____

_____

_____

_____

_____

_____

_____

_____

_____

_____

_____

How did your dad, my grandpa, affect you as a mom?

Do you feel like a good mother?

_____

_____

_____

_____

_____

_____

_____

_____

_____

_____

_____

_____

_____

_____

_____

_____

_____

_____

_____

FAMILY FACES ARE MAGIC
MIRRORS. LOOKING AT
PEOPLE WHO BELONG TO US
WE SEE THE PAST, PRESENT, &
FUTURE. ♥ *Gail Lumet Buckley*

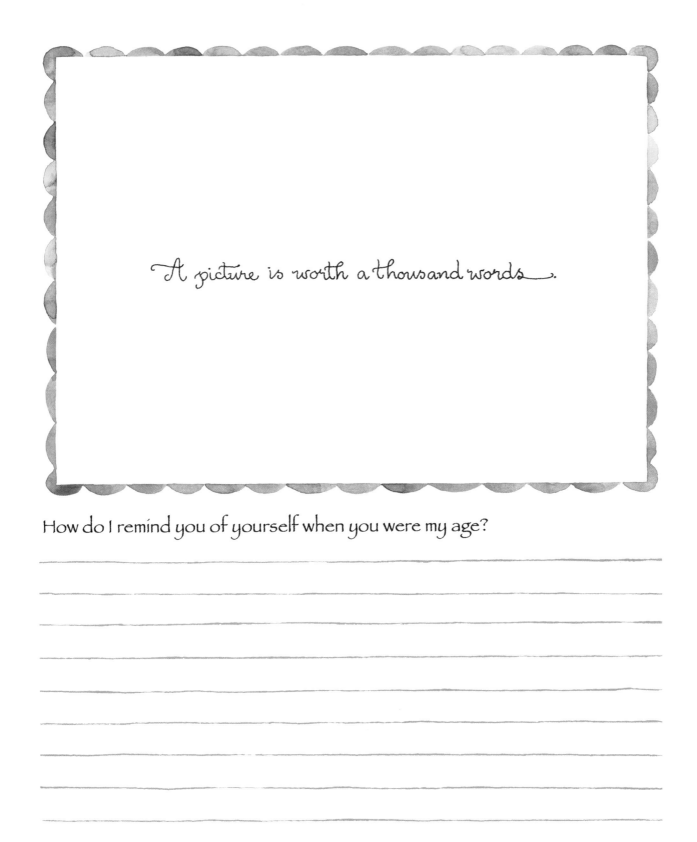

A picture is worth a thousand words.

How do I remind you of yourself when you were my age?

_____
_____
_____
_____
_____
_____
_____
_____
_____
_____
_____
_____

Do you miss having little children?

How did it feel when I moved away from home?

What should I know about having children?

All about you...

What do you love to do?

What is your favorite flower?

_____

_____

_____

_____

_____

_____

_____

_____

_____

What is your favorite quote?

_____

_____

_____

_____

_____

_____

_____

_____

_____

_____

_____

_____

Write down a favorite family recipe. Where did you get it?

_____

_____

_____

_____

_____

_____

_____

_____

_____

_____

_____

_____

_____

_____

_____

_____

_____

_____

_____

If you could be any age again, which would you choose?

_____

_____

_____

_____

_____

_____

_____

_____

_____

_____

_____

_____

_____

_____

_____

_____

_____

_____

_____

_____

_____

"Backward, turn backward, O Time in your flight;
Make me a child again just for tonight." ♥

Elizabeth Akers Allen

Where have you traveled that you loved the best? Tell me why.

What's the best place you have ever lived?

_____

_____

_____

_____

_____

_____

_____

_____

_____

_____

_____

_____

_____

_____

_____

_____

_____

_____

_____

_____

_____

_____

A house is made of walls & beams; a home is built with love & dreams.

What's your secret food addiction?

_____

_____

_____

_____

_____

_____

_____

_____

_____

_____

_____

_____

_____

_____

_____

_____

_____

_____

"THINGS TASTE
BETTER
IN
SMALL HOUSES."
Queen Victoria

What's a favorite piece of jewelry you own? Where did you get it?

_____

_____

_____

_____

_____

_____

_____

_____

_____

_____

_____

_____

_____

_____

_____

_____

_____

_____

_____

I BELIEVE
IN
ACCESSORIES

What was the most surprising gift you ever received?

The best gifts are tied with heartstrings.

Who are your heroes?

If you could do it all over, would you change anything?

What would you most like to be remembered for?

_____
_____
_____
_____
_____
_____
_____
_____
_____
_____
_____
_____
_____
_____
_____
_____
_____
_____
_____

YOU ONLY LIVE ONCE BUT IF YOU WORK IT RIGHT, ONCE IS ENOUGH.

What advice about life would you love to give but know I don't want to hear?

_____

_____

_____

_____

_____

_____

_____

_____

_____

_____

_____

_____

_____

_____

_____

_____

_____

_____

_____

_____

_____

What makes you happiest?

A JOY SHARED IS A JOY DOUBLED

What is the most important thing you have learned?

THE BEST THINGS IN LIFE AREN'T THINGS. ♡

More stories...

A picture goes here;
your family, your house,
your dog, your cat —
but best would be
YOU
since this is your book. ♥

Never underestimate the value

of the little moment ♡.

_____

Sign your name

_____

Date

♥